MRJC
09/19

Watch a Pineapple Grow

by Kirsten Chang

Ideas for Parents and Teachers

Bullfrog Books let children practice reading informational text at the earliest reading levels. Repetition, familiar words, and photo labels support early readers.

Before Reading

- Discuss the cover photo. What does it tell them?

- Look at the picture glossary together. Read and discuss the words.

Read the Book

- "Walk" through the book and look at the photos. Let the child ask questions. Point out the photo labels.

- Read the book to the child, or have him or her read independently.

After Reading

- Prompt the child to think more. Ask: Do you like to eat pineapples? Can you explain how they grow?

Bullfrog Books are published by Jump!
5357 Penn Avenue South
Minneapolis, MN 55419
www.jumplibrary.com

Library of Congress Cataloging-in-Publication Data

Names: Chang, Kirsten, author.
Title: Watch a pineapple grow / by Kirsten Chang.
Description: Minneapolis, MN: Jump!, Inc., [2019]
Series: Bullfrog books. Watch it grow
Audience: Ages 5-8.
Includes bibliographical references and index.
Identifiers: LCCN 2018019332 (print)
LCCN 2018020427 (ebook)
ISBN 9781641282604 (ebook)
ISBN 9781641282581 (hardcover: alk. paper)
ISBN 9781641282598 (pbk.)
Subjects: LCSH: Pineapple—Growth—
Juvenile literature. | CYAC: Pineapple.
Classification: LCC SB375 (ebook)
LCC SB375 .C43 2018 (print) | DDC 634/.774—dc23
LC record available at https://lccn.loc.gov/2018019332

Editor: Jenna Trnka
Designer: Michelle Sonnek

Photo Credits: Max Lashcheuski/Shutterstock, cover (pineapple); Jan Havlicek/Shutterstock, cover (plant); fotostorm/iStock, 1; ifong/Shutterstock, 3; ktaylorg/iStock, 4 (girl); Ivica Drusany/Shutterstock, 4 (background); eWilding/Shutterstock, 5; showcake/Shutterstock, 6, 22t; Monrudee/Shutterstock, 7, 22mr; tanewpix/Shutterstock, 8–9, 23br; KANIT TEEBET/Shutterstock, 10–11, 22br; jipatafoto89/Shutterstock, 12–13; NATTHAPHONG PHRACHAN/Shutterstock, 14–15, 22bl; 9comeback/Shutterstock, 16–17, 22ml, 23tl; Marco Simoni/Getty, 18; Petr Student/Shutterstock, 19 (truck), 23tr; Evlakhov Law Gavel/Shutterstock, 19 (pineapples), 23bl; Alon Othnay/Shutterstock, 20–21; Buntoon Rodseng/Shutterstock, 23bl; Tim UR/Shutterstock, 24.

Printed in the United States of America at Corporate Graphics in North Mankato, Minnesota.

Table of Contents

Leafy Top

Nel loves pineapple.

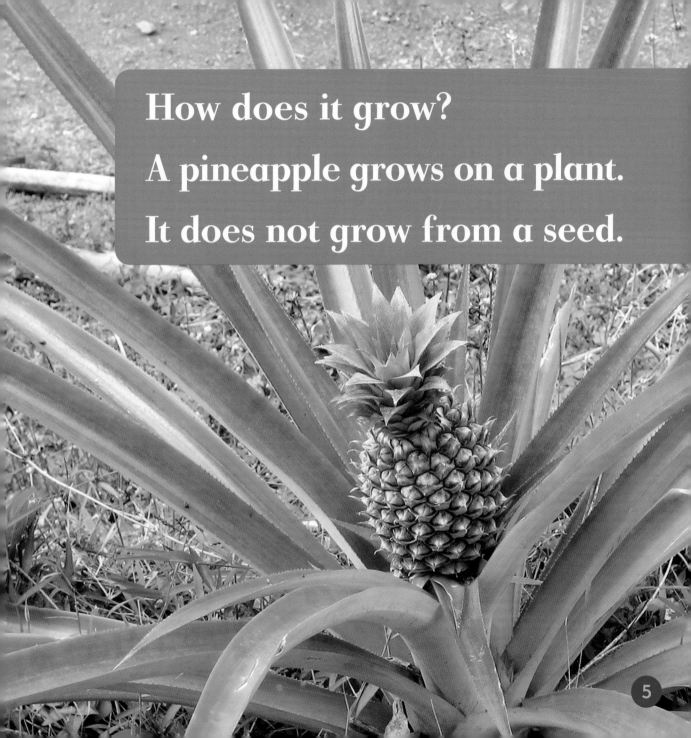

How does it grow?

A pineapple grows on a plant.

It does not grow from a seed.

A farmer
takes part of
an old plant.

A new plant grows from it.

soil

What does it
need to grow?

Sandy soil.

Sunshine.

Warmth.

The plant grows many flowers.

flower

The flowers grow.
They start to
stick together.

This makes a fruit.

fruit

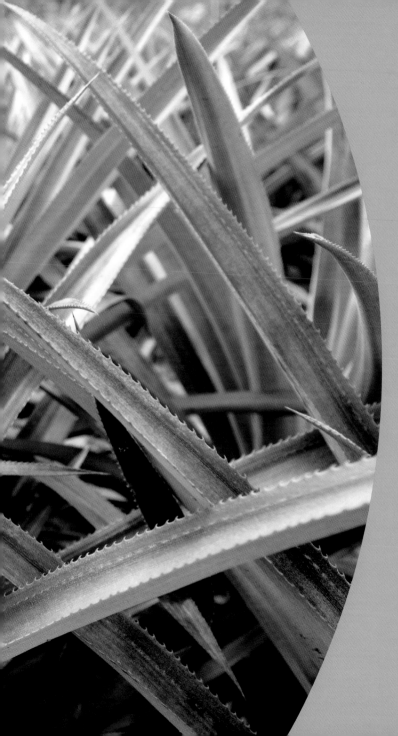

Is it ready to
be picked?

Yes!

It is yellow.

It is ripe.

17

Farmers cut each pineapple from the plant.

18

They are shipped away.

We buy one at the grocery store.

We love pineapple!

Life Cycle of a Pineapple

How does a pineapple grow?

pineapple part

plant

flowers

fruit

ripe pineapple

Picture Glossary

ripe
Fully grown and ready to eat.

shipped
Sent from one place to another.

soil
Another word for dirt.

warmth
The state of being warm in temperature.

Index

To Learn More

Learning more is as easy as 1, 2, 3.

1) Go to www.factsurfer.com

2) Enter "watchapineapplegrow" into the search box.

3) Click the "Surf" button to see a list of websites.

With factsurfer.com, finding more information is just a click away.